MUSLIM
Gratitude
JOURNAL

THIS BOOK BELONGS TO

Thank you for purchasing this book!

We wish you well on your journey to an

attitude of gratitude mindset!

Definition of Gratitude

[grat-i-tood, -tyood]

THE QUALITY OR FEELING OF BEING GRATEFUL OR THANKFUL

Synonyms
thanks, thankfulness, appreciation, gratefulness.

Origin
1400-50; late Middle English < Medieval Latin grātitūdin- (stem of grātitūdō)
thankfulness, equivalent to grāt(us) pleasing + -i- -i- + -tūdin- -tude

Tips for Maintaining a Gratitude Journal

1. Schedule a time in your daily calendar to write in your journal and set a digital reminder on your phone. Before bed is a fantastic time so you can reflect on the day.

2. Write as many things that come to mind. You can keep the list simple with just a few words, or elaborate to your hearts content. Do what works best for you.

3. Put aside all distractions (phones, tv, spouse) and be conscious of the words that you're writing.

4. Be consistent. Some days you will feel there's not much to be grateful for. This is when you need to dig deeper. Really think about what it is that you're grateful for. These occasions help uncover true hidden gems in our lives that we sometimes don't see or ignore.

5. Finally, focussing on people, rather than things, helps build *unbelievably* strong relationships in your life.

Why be Thankful?

As Muslims, we are encouraged to have an attitude of gratitude, not only towards our Creator, but also towards those around us.

It's amazing the amount of benefit, both spiritually and mentally, that comes from being grateful for the small and big things in our day-to-day lives.

Below, we will share some Quranic verses and narrations from our Prophet relating to the topic of gratitude and thankfulness:

"And [remember] when your Lord proclaimed,
'If you are grateful, I will surely increase you [in favor];
but if you deny, indeed, My punishment is severe."
Ibrahim 14:7

"We bestowed wisdom on Luqman:
'Show gratitude to God. Anyone who is grateful
does so to profit his own soul: but whoever
is ungrateful verily God is free of all
wants worthy of praise.'"
Luqman 31:12

"And whatever of blessings and good
things you have, it is from God"
An-Nahl 16:53

"*Then when (Solomon) saw it placed before him
[referring to the throne of the Queen of Sheba],
he said: 'This is by the Grace of my Lord to test me
whether I am grateful or ungrateful! And whoever is
grateful, truly, his gratitude is for (the good of) his
own self, and whoever is ungrateful, (he is ungrateful
only for the loss of his own self). Certainly! My Lord
is Rich (Free of all wants), Bountiful.'*"
An-Naml 27:40

Prophet Muhammad (Peace Be Upon Him) said,
"*He who does not thank people, does not thank God*"
Ahmad, Tirmidhi

Prophet Muhammad (Peace Be Upon Him) said,
"*Whoever does you a favor, then reciprocate, and if you cannot find
anything with which to reciprocate, then pray for that person until you
think that you have reciprocated them.*"
Abu Dawood

My Week Of Gratitude

Call upon me, I will respond to you
Ghafir 40:60

Today I am grateful for: | |

_____

_____

_____

_____

Today I am grateful for: | |

_____

_____

_____

_____

Today I am grateful for: | |

_____

_____

_____

_____

Today I am grateful for: | |

Today I am grateful for: | |

Today I am grateful for: | |

Today I am grateful for: | |

    9

My Week Of Gratitude

If you are grateful, I will surely increase you [in favor]
Ibrahim 14:7

Today I am grateful for: | |

Today I am grateful for: | |

Today I am grateful for: | |

Today I am grateful for: | |

Today I am grateful for: | |

Today I am grateful for: | |

Today I am grateful for: | |

 11

What is one thing in your life that makes
you want to especially thank Allah and why?

| | |

_____

_____

_____

_____

_____

_____

_____

_____

_____

_____

_____

_____

_____

My Deep Inner Thoughts & Reflections:

| |

My Week Of Gratitude

My mercy embraces all things
Al-A'raf 7:156

Today I am grateful for: | |

Today I am grateful for: | |

Today I am grateful for: | |

Today I am grateful for: | |

Today I am grateful for: | |

Today I am grateful for: | |

Today I am grateful for: | |

My Week Of Gratitude

My success can only come from Allah
Hud 11:88

Today I am grateful for: | |

Today I am grateful for: | |

Today I am grateful for: | |

Today I am grateful for: | |

_____
_____
_____
_____

Today I am grateful for: | |

_____
_____
_____
_____

Today I am grateful for: | |

_____
_____
_____
_____

Today I am grateful for: | |

_____
_____
_____
_____

When was the last time you visited someone sick?
How did it make them feel? Also, how did you feel?

/ /

My Deep Inner Thoughts & Reflections:

| |

My Week Of Gratitude

*The good **deed** and the bad deed **are not** the same. **Return evil** with good*
Fussilat 41:34

Today I am grateful for: | |

Today I am grateful for: | |

Today I am grateful for: | |

Today I am grateful for: | |

Today I am grateful for: | |

Today I am grateful for: | |

Today I am grateful for: | |

     21

My Week Of Gratitude

Allah does not burden a soul beyond that it can bear
Al-Baqarah 2:286

Today I am grateful for: | |

Today I am grateful for: | |

Today I am grateful for: | |

Today I am grateful for: | |

Today I am grateful for: | |

Today I am grateful for: | |

Today I am grateful for: | |

Describe a recent time when you truly felt at peace:

_____ / _____ / _____

My Deep Inner Thoughts & Reflections:

/ /

My Week Of Gratitude

So be patient. Indeed, the promise of Allah is truth
Ar-Rum 30:60

Today I am grateful for:

Today I am grateful for:

Today I am grateful for:

Today I am grateful for: | |

Today I am grateful for: | |

Today I am grateful for: | |

Today I am grateful for: | |

My Week Of Gratitude

Indeed, Allah is with those who fear Him and those who are doers of good
An-Nahl 16:128

Today I am grateful for: | |

Today I am grateful for: | |

Today I am grateful for: | |

Today I am grateful for: | |

Today I am grateful for: | |

Today I am grateful for: | |

Today I am grateful for: | |

What is your favorite verse in the Qur'an and why?

/ /

My Deep Inner Thoughts & Reflections:

/ /

My Week Of Gratitude

Hold firmly to the rope of Allah
Ali 'Imran 3:103

Today I am grateful for: | |

Today I am grateful for: | |

Today I am grateful for: | |

Today I am grateful for: | |

Today I am grateful for: | |

Today I am grateful for: | |

Today I am grateful for: | |

 33

My Week Of Gratitude

Indeed! The Help of Allah is near
Al-Baqarah 2:214

Today I am grateful for: | |

Today I am grateful for: | |

Today I am grateful for: | |

Today I am grateful for: | |

Today I am grateful for: | |

Today I am grateful for: | |

Today I am grateful for: | |

Describe a sunnah that you adhere to
regularly which brings you joy?

/ /

My Deep Inner Thoughts & Reflections:

_____ / _____ / _____

My Week Of Gratitude

And whoever puts all his trust in Allah He will be enough for him
At-Talaq 65:3

Today I am grateful for | |

Today I am grateful for | |

Today I am grateful for | |

Today I am grateful for: | |

Today I am grateful for: | |

Today I am grateful for: | |

Today I am grateful for: | |

 39

My Week Of Gratitude

And your Lord says, "Call upon Me; I will respond to you"
Ghafir 40:80

Today I am grateful for:

Today I am grateful for:

Today I am grateful for:

Today I am grateful for: | |

Today I am grateful for: | |

Today I am grateful for: | |

Today I am grateful for: | |

 41

Write one deed you do on a regular basis that no one else knows about, and how it makes you feel?

My Deep Inner Thoughts & Reflections:

| |

My Week Of Gratitude

And if you would count the graces of Allah, never would you be able to count them
Ibrahim 14:34

Today I am grateful for: | |

Today I am grateful for: | |

Today I am grateful for: | |

Today I am grateful for: | |

Today I am grateful for: | |

Today I am grateful for: | |

Today I am grateful for: | |

 45

My Week Of Gratitude

Do not despair of the mercy of Allah
Az-Zumar 39:53

Today I am grateful for: | |

Today I am grateful for: | |

Today I am grateful for: | |

Today I am grateful for:

Today I am grateful for:

Today I am grateful for:

Today I am grateful for:

 47

What good character traits can you learn
from 5 people you know?

My Deep Inner Thoughts & Reflections:

| | |

My Week Of Gratitude

Indeed, Allah forgives all sins
Az-Zumar 39:53

Today I am grateful for: | |

Today I am grateful for: | |

Today I am grateful for: | |

Today I am grateful for: | |

Today I am grateful for: | |

Today I am grateful for: | |

Today I am grateful for: | |

 51

My Week Of Gratitude

Allah is the light of the Heavens and the Earth
An-Nur 24:35

Today I am grateful for | |

Today I am grateful for | |

Today I am grateful for | |

Today I am grateful for: | |

Today I am grateful for: | |

Today I am grateful for: | |

Today I am grateful for: | |

 53

Which is the easiest daily prayer to perform and why is it so easy for you? And which is the hardest and what makes it difficult?

My Deep Inner Thoughts & Reflections:

| | |

_____

_____

_____

_____

_____

_____

_____

_____

_____

_____

_____

_____

_____

_____

_____

_____

_____

_____

_____

_____

My Week Of Gratitude

Indeed, Allah is ever Knowing and Wise
Al-Insan 76:30

Today I am grateful for: | |

Today I am grateful for: | |

Today I am grateful for: | |

Today I am grateful for: | |

Today I am grateful for: | |

Today I am grateful for: | |

Today I am grateful for: | |

My Week Of Gratitude

Indeed what is to come will be better for you than what has gone by
Ad-Duhaa 93:4

Today I am grateful for:

Today I am grateful for:

Today I am grateful for:

Today I am grateful for: | |

Today I am grateful for: | |

Today I am grateful for: | |

Today I am grateful for: | |

     59

When was the last time you felt complete
concentration in your salah? What steps
could you take to regain that feeling?

| |

_____
_____
_____
_____
_____
_____
_____
_____
_____
_____
_____
_____
_____
_____

My Deep Inner Thoughts & Reflections:

| |

My Week Of Gratitude

Do good to your parents
Al-Isra 17:23

Today I am grateful for | |

Today I am grateful for | |

Today I am grateful for | |

Today I am grateful for: | |

Today I am grateful for: | |

Today I am grateful for: | |

Today I am grateful for: | |

   63

My Week Of Gratitude

Verily, Allah forgives all sins
Az-Zumar 39:53

Today I am grateful for | |

Today I am grateful for | |

Today I am grateful for | |

Today I am grateful for: | |

Today I am grateful for: | |

Today I am grateful for: | |

Today I am grateful for: | |

Describe a blessing of Allah that
you are most grateful for?

My Deep Inner Thoughts & Reflections:

| |

_____
_____
_____
_____
_____
_____
_____
_____
_____
_____
_____
_____
_____
_____
_____
_____
_____
_____

My Week Of Gratitude

So endure patiently, with beautiful patience
Al-Ma'arij 70:5

Today I am grateful for: | |

Today I am grateful for: | |

Today I am grateful for: | |

Today I am grateful for: | |

Today I am grateful for: | |

Today I am grateful for: | |

Today I am grateful for: | |

My Week Of Gratitude

Do not be afraid; I am with you all the time, listening and seeing
Taha 20:46

Today I am grateful for: | |

Today I am grateful for: | |

Today I am grateful for: | |

Today I am grateful for: | |

Today I am grateful for: | |

Today I am grateful for: | |

Today I am grateful for: | |

What is the biggest life lesson you've
learned as a Muslim?

My Deep Inner Thoughts & Reflections:

| | |

My Week Of Gratitude

And to Allah belongs the outcome of all matters
Al-Haj 22:41

Today I am grateful for: | |

Today I am grateful for: | |

Today I am grateful for: | |

14

Today I am grateful for: | |

Today I am grateful for: | |

Today I am grateful for: | |

Today I am grateful for: | |

My Week Of Gratitude

And establish prayer; surely prayer keeps one away from indecency and evil
Al-'Ankabut 29:45

Today I am grateful for: | |

Today I am grateful for: | |

Today I am grateful for: | |

Today I am grateful for: | |

Today I am grateful for: | |

Today I am grateful for: | |

Today I am grateful for: | |

When was the last time you gave a gift to someone without expecting anything in return? How did it make you feel?

| | |

My Deep Inner Thoughts & Reflections:

| |

My Week Of Gratitude

Every soul will taste death
Ali 'Imran 3:185

Today I am grateful for: | |

Today I am grateful for: | |

Today I am grateful for: | |

Today I am grateful for: | |

Today I am grateful for: | |

Today I am grateful for: | |

Today I am grateful for: | |

 81

My Week Of Gratitude

And do not let your dislike of a people lead you to be unjust
Al-Ma-idah 5:8

Today I am grateful for: | |

Today I am grateful for: | |

Today I am grateful for: | |

Today I am grateful for: | |

Today I am grateful for: | |

Today I am grateful for: | |

Today I am grateful for: | |

 83

List 10 blessings in your life that
you can thank Allah for:

| | |

My Deep Inner Thoughts & Reflections:

| | |

My Week Of Gratitude

Indeed, my Lord is near and responsive
Hud 11:61

Today I am grateful for:

Today I am grateful for:

Today I am grateful for:

Today I am grateful for: | |

Today I am grateful for: | |

Today I am grateful for: | |

Today I am grateful for: | |

 87

My Week Of Gratitude

There is no compulsion in religion
Al-Baqarah 2:256

Today I am grateful for: | |

Today I am grateful for: | |

Today I am grateful for: | |

Today I am grateful for: | |

Today I am grateful for: | |

Today I am grateful for: | |

Today I am grateful for: | |

 89

Who is a friend you can count on and why?

| | |

My Deep Inner Thoughts & Reflections:

| | |

My Week Of Gratitude

If you are grateful, I will give you more
Ibrahim 14:7

Today I am grateful for: | |

Today I am grateful for: | |

Today I am grateful for: | |

Today I am grateful for: | |

Today I am grateful for: | |

Today I am grateful for: | |

Today I am grateful for: | |

 93

My Week Of Gratitude

No person knows what he will earn tomorrow
Luqman 31:34

Today I am grateful for: | |

Today I am grateful for: | |

Today I am grateful for: | |

Today I am grateful for: | |

Today I am grateful for: | |

Today I am grateful for: | |

Today I am grateful for: | |

       95

Think of the five people in your life whom you spend
the most time with. Are they helping or hurting
your chances of achieving your goals in life?

My Deep Inner Thoughts & Reflections:

| |

My Week Of Gratitude

And We have certainly beautified the nearest heaven with stars
At-Talaq 67:5

Today I am grateful for: | |

Today I am grateful for: | |

Today I am grateful for: | |

Today I am grateful for: | |

Today I am grateful for: | |

Today I am grateful for: | |

Today I am grateful for: | |

My Week Of Gratitude

And We created you in pairs
An-Naba 78:8

Today I am grateful for: | |

Today I am grateful for: | |

Today I am grateful for: | |

Today I am grateful for: | |

Today I am grateful for: | |

Today I am grateful for: | |

Today I am grateful for: | |

What is your favorite hadith and
what makes it so special to you?

| |

My Deep Inner Thoughts & Reflections:

| | |

My Week Of Gratitude

"And He is with you wherever you are"
Al-Hadid 57:4

Today I am grateful for: | |

Today I am grateful for: | |

Today I am grateful for: | |

Today I am grateful for: | |

Today I am grateful for: | |

Today I am grateful for: | |

Today I am grateful for: | |

 105

My Week Of Gratitude

And Allah is the best of providers
Al-Jumu'ah 62:11

Today I am grateful for: | |

Today I am grateful for: | |

Today I am grateful for: | |

Today I am grateful for: | |

Today I am grateful for: | |

Today I am grateful for: | |

Today I am grateful for: | |

Describe 5 things you have that others around the world may not have?

| | |

My Week Of Gratitude

This is the book about which there is no doubt, a guidance for those conscious of Allah
Al-Baqarah 2:2

Today I am grateful for:

Today I am grateful for:

Today I am grateful for:

Today I am grateful for: | |

Today I am grateful for: | |

Today I am grateful for: | |

Today I am grateful for: | |

My Week Of Gratitude

The life of this world is only the enjoyment of deception
Ali 'Imran 3:185

Today I am grateful for: | |

Today I am grateful for: | |

Today I am grateful for: | |

Today I am grateful for: | |

Today I am grateful for: | |

Today I am grateful for: | |

Today I am grateful for: | |

 113

When was the last time you committed a sin
without feeling any guilt and why?

/   /

My Deep Inner Thoughts & Reflections:

| |

My Week Of Gratitude

Indeed, Prayer prohibits immorality and wrongdoing
Al-'Ankabut 29:45

Today I am grateful for: | |

Today I am grateful for: | |

Today I am grateful for: | |

Today I am grateful for: | |

Today I am grateful for: | |

Today I am grateful for: | |

Today I am grateful for: | |

 117

My Week Of Gratitude

And worship your Lord until there comes unto you the certainty (death)
Al-Hijr 15:99

Today I am grateful for: | |

Today I am grateful for: | |

Today I am grateful for: | |

Today I am grateful for: | |

Today I am grateful for: | |

Today I am grateful for: | |

Today I am grateful for: | |

 119

How would it make you feel to enter Jannah?
Describe your emotions in detail:

/   /

My Week Of Gratitude

And ask for forgiveness of your Lord and repent to Him. Indeed, my Lord is merciful and loving
Hud 11:90

Today I am grateful for:

Today I am grateful for:

Today I am grateful for:

Today I am grateful for: | |

Today I am grateful for: | |

Today I am grateful for: | |

Today I am grateful for: | |

My Week Of Gratitude

Do what is beautiful. Allah loves those who do what is beautiful
Baqarah 2:195

Today I am grateful for: | |

Today I am grateful for: | |

Today I am grateful for: | |

Today I am grateful for: | |

_____

_____

_____

_____

Today I am grateful for: | |

_____

_____

_____

_____

Today I am grateful for: | |

_____

_____

_____

_____

Today I am grateful for: | |

_____

_____

_____

_____

When was the last time you sat down after salah
to remember Allah with sincere dua or dhikr?

| |

My Deep Inner Thoughts & Reflections:

| |

My Week Of Gratitude

So verily, with the hardship, there is relief. Verily, with the hardship, there is relief
Ash-Sharh 94:5-6

Today I am grateful for: | |

Today I am grateful for: | |

Today I am grateful for: | |

Today I am grateful for: | |

Today I am grateful for: | |

Today I am grateful for: | |

Today I am grateful for: | |

My Week Of Gratitude

Our Lord! Forgive me and my parents, and (all) the believers on
the Day when the reckoning will be established
Ibrahim 14:41

Today I am grateful for:　　　　　　　　　　|　　　|

Today I am grateful for:　　　　　　　　　　|　　　|

Today I am grateful for:　　　　　　　　　　|　　　|

Today I am grateful for: | |

Today I am grateful for: | |

Today I am grateful for: | |

Today I am grateful for: | |

Why do you call yourself a Muslim?

/ /

My Deep Inner Thoughts & Reflections:

| | |

My Week Of Gratitude

So remember me; I will remember you
Al-Baqarah 2:152

Today I am grateful for:　　　|　　|

Today I am grateful for:　　　|　　|

Today I am grateful for:　　　|　　|

Today I am grateful for: | |

Today I am grateful for: | |

Today I am grateful for: | |

Today I am grateful for: | |

 135

My Week Of Gratitude

And whoever puts all his trust in Allah, He will be enough for him
At-Talaq 65:1-3

Today I am grateful for: | |

Today I am grateful for: | |

Today I am grateful for: | |

Today I am grateful for: | |

Today I am grateful for: | |

Today I am grateful for: | |

Today I am grateful for: | |

When was the last time you felt jealous
of someone else and why?

| |

| | |

My Week Of Gratitude

It may be that you dislike a thing which is good for you and that you like a thing which is bad for you. Allah knows but you do not know
Al-Baqarah 2:216

Today I am grateful for:

Today I am grateful for:

Today I am grateful for:

Today I am grateful for: | |

Today I am grateful for: | |

Today I am grateful for: | |

Today I am grateful for: | |

My Week Of Gratitude

And who despairs from the mercy of his Lord, except those astray?
Al-Hijr 15:56

Today I am grateful for: | |

Today I am grateful for: | |

Today I am grateful for: | |

Today I am grateful for: | |

Today I am grateful for: | |

Today I am grateful for: | |

Today I am grateful for: | |

 143

Write down 10 things you would love to
have, see or do in Jannah?

_____ / _____ / _____

| | |

My Week Of Gratitude

And all will come to Him on the day of Resurrection alone
Maryam 19:95

Today I am grateful for: | |

Today I am grateful for: | |

Today I am grateful for: | |

Today I am grateful for: | |

Today I am grateful for: | |

Today I am grateful for: | |

Today I am grateful for: | |

        147

My Week Of Gratitude

You prefer the life of this world, while the hereafter is better & more lasting
Al-A'la 87:16

Today I am grateful for: | |

Today I am grateful for: | |

Today I am grateful for: | |

Today I am grateful for: | |

Today I am grateful for: | |

Today I am grateful for: | |

Today I am grateful for: | |

When was the last time you spoke ill about
someone behind their back and why?

| |

My Deep Inner Thoughts & Reflections:

/ /

My Week Of Gratitude

But they plan, and Allah plans. And Allah is the best of planners
Ali 'Imran 3:54

Today I am grateful for: | |

Today I am grateful for: | |

Today I am grateful for: | |

Today I am grateful for: | |

Today I am grateful for: | |

Today I am grateful for: | |

Today I am grateful for: | |

My Week Of Gratitude

Whoever does righteousness, male or female, while believing, we will grant them a happy life
An-Nahl 16:97

Today I am grateful for: /   /

```
---------------------------------------------------------------
---------------------------------------------------------------
---------------------------------------------------------------
---------------------------------------------------------------
```

Today I am grateful for: /   /

```
---------------------------------------------------------------
---------------------------------------------------------------
---------------------------------------------------------------
---------------------------------------------------------------
```

Today I am grateful for: /   /

```
---------------------------------------------------------------
---------------------------------------------------------------
---------------------------------------------------------------
---------------------------------------------------------------
```

Today I am grateful for: | |

Today I am grateful for: | |

Today I am grateful for: | |

Today I am grateful for: | |

 155

Have you ever argued with someone even though, in your heart, you knew you were wrong and why?

| |

My Deep Inner Thoughts & Reflections:

My Week Of Gratitude

So let not this present life deceive you
Fatir 35:5

Today I am grateful for:

Today I am grateful for:

Today I am grateful for:

Today I am grateful for | |

Today I am grateful for | |

Today I am grateful for | |

Today I am grateful for | |

My Week Of Gratitude

We will test you in fear, hunger, loss of wealth, life and fruit, but give glad tidings to the patient
Al-Baqarah 2:155

Today I am grateful for: | |

Today I am grateful for: | |

Today I am grateful for: | |

Today I am grateful for: | |

Today I am grateful for: | |

Today I am grateful for: | |

Today I am grateful for: | |

  161

Describe one good deed you want to implement in your life which would help to increase your level of emaan?

| |

_____
_____
_____
_____
_____
_____
_____
_____
_____
_____
_____
_____
_____
_____
_____
_____
_____

My Deep Inner Thoughts & Reflections:

| / | / |

Bonus Questions

When was the last time you smiled at someone with a clean heart knowing that a smile is an act of charity?

When was the last time you opened the Qur'an to read one page? If it was a long time ago, why do you think that is?

What steps can you take to improve your relationship with Allah?

Made in the USA
Coppell, TX
15 September 2022